A Kalmus Classic Edition

Orlando

GIBBONS

AN ALBUM OF POPULAR PIECES

FOR PIANO

K 03470

Orlando Gibbons.
(1583 - 1625.)

There is scarcely a name in ecclesiastical musical history better known or more frequently quoted than that of Orlando Gibbons. At the same time it must be acknowledged that there are few about whose works so little is known, or regarding whom so little information can be gleaned from presumably trustworthy sources. Even the latest biographical notice prefixed by Sir Frederick A. G. Ouseley to a recent collection of some of his Church music does not add a single fact not already familiar, and makes no attempt to settle the question still in dispute as to the certainty of the date and place of his early academical honours. It is enough, however, for posterity that his works exist, and by and for these, is he allowed an honourable place in the Walhalla of musical literature, not simply because of the number and character of those productions alone, but because of the influence of his advanced turn of thought, and the graceful treatment of scientific means which is one is of the most striking peculiarities of all his works, sacred and secular, vocal and instrumental. Orlando Gibbons was born at Cambridge in the year 1583, and displayed such early promise of ability that at the age of twenty-one—namely, in the year 1604—he was appointed to one of the then much coveted places in Chapel Royal, taking his turn according to his " waiting," as the attendance on duty is called, to preside at the organ. He commenced his career as a composer at a very early age, producing " fantaisies for viols," madrigals, songs, and other vocal pieces, as well as music for the virginals in great variety. He was associated with Byrde and Bull in the publication of " Parthenia," the first book of collected original pieces for the instrument just named. This work was engraved on and printed from copper plates, as was stated in the preface, and was long supposed to be the first work of the kind so treated; but subsequent research has proved this to be an error, as a work of earlier date was issued in Italy. The discovery of this fact in no way detracts from the merit of either of the compositions which appear in the book, but on the contrary it shows that whatever may have been the state of art and the means of multiplying copies, that English composers of that period were in 'no respect inferior to their continental compeers in their inventive or executive skill, for although the pieces are not easy even for modern players, it may be assumed that the composers themselves were able to perform their own productions. Of the sacred music of Orlando Gibbons, much might be said if occasion needed. It must suffice here to state, as a proof of their present popularity, that scarcely a day passes upon which one or other of his services or anthems is not performed in some of the cathedral or collegiate churches in this kingdom. An eight-part anthem of his composition, " O clap your hands," which is still frequently sung, was the work written in 1622 as the exercise for the degree of Doctor in Music conferred by the University of Oxford upon William Heyther, the founder of the Professorial Chair of Music, at which time also Gibbons is said to have received the like honour, which unfortunately, he did not live long to enjoy. In 1625 he was commanded by King Charles to attend in his train from London to Dover, at which place the Queen Henrietta was expected to land from France. While on the journey, in the city of Canterbury, Gibbons was seized with an attack of small-pox, of which he died, being in his forty-fifth year. He was buried with all due respect to his position and attainments in the cathedral, and a monument was placed in the nave to commemorate the musician, who, by his works, still speaks and stirs the hearts of worshippers to reverence and devotion, and of musicians to emulation and imitation.

Orlando Gibbons.
(1583-1625.)
Preludium.

(cresc.)
(f)
(f)
(p)
(<　　>)
(f)

Galiardo.

(II.)
(Variation.)
(III.)

(Variation.)

Fantazia of foure Parts.

The Lord of Salisbury his Pavin.

Galiardo.

67
(II)
(Variation.)

(III.)
(Variation.)

The Queenes Command.

(p)
(f)